ANIMAL ARMIES

CHIMPANZEE TROOPS

RICHARD AND
LOUISE SPILSBURY

PowerKiDS
press
New York

Published in 2013 by The Rosen Publishing Group, Inc.
29 East 21st Street, New York, NY 10010

Produced for Rosen by Calcium Creative Ltd
Editors for Calcium Creative Ltd: Sarah Eason and Katie Woolley
US Editor: Sara Antill
Designers: Paul Myerscough and Geoff Ward

Photo credits: Dreamstime: Alterfalter 20–21, Sergey Uryadnikov 24; Shutterstock: Aaron Amat 16–17, Nick Biemans 12–13, Norma Cornes 13, Sam D Cruz 10–11, Kristof Degreef 14, Boris Diakovsky 16, EML 5, Fashcool 28, Eric Gevaert 1, 23, Chris Humphries 27, Alan Jeffery 22–23, Jurie Maree 18–19, Meawpong3405 26–27, Stephen Meese 4–5, Sharon Morris 14–15, Neelsky 7, Uryadnikov Sergey 9, 10, 28–29, Tiago Jorge da Silva Estima 18, Smileus 20, Y F Wong cover, XAOC 8–9, Zebra0209 24–25, Alessandro Zocc 6–7.

Library of Congress Cataloging-in-Publication Data

Spilsbury, Richard, 1963–
 Chimpanzee troops / by Richard Spilsbury and Louise Spilsbury.
    p. cm. — (Animal armies)
 Includes index.
 ISBN 978-1-4777-0303-8 (library binding) — ISBN 978-1-4777-0328-1 (pbk.) —
ISBN 978-1-4777-0329-8 (6-pack)
 1. Chimpanzees—Behavior—Juvenile literature. 2. Social behavior in animals—Juvenile literature. I. Spilsbury, Louise. II. Title.
 QL737.P96S643 2013
 599.885—dc23

                                      2012019586

Manufactured in the United States of America

CPSIA Compliance Information: Batch #W13PK2: For Further Information contact Rosen Publishing, New York, New York at 1-800-237-9932

CONTENTS

CHIMPANZEES

Chimpanzees are **apes** that live in and around trees in parts of Africa. They are strong, smart animals. They have no tails, but they do have long arms and fingers. Chimpanzees use these to climb up trees and swing from branch to branch.

A group of chimpanzees is called a troop. The number of chimpanzees in a troop varies from one group to another. One chimpanzee troop can have as few as 10 or 15 chimpanzees. Other troops can have as many as 120 animals. Just like the soldiers in an army, chimpanzees feed, work, and play with the other members of their troop. Being part of a team helps each chimpanzee in the group to survive.

Chimpanzees can march quickly on all fours or on two legs.

All the chimpanzees in a troop know each other. They feed, travel, and sleep in small groups of six or fewer.

Fight to Survive

Chimpanzees live in a troop to **protect** themselves. Being part of a group helps to keep these animals safe from **predators**.

RANK

In an army, soldiers have different **ranks**. There are leaders and followers. There is only one leader in a troop of chimpanzees. This is the **alpha** male. He becomes the boss of the group by protecting the troop and by fighting and **defeating** other males.

The other chimpanzees in a troop have different ranks, too. Adult males are of a higher rank than adult females. Older females are **dominant** over younger females. Young chimpanzees have the lowest rank of all! Young chimpanzees always look down when they meet the leader of the troop, to show they know that he is the boss.

The leader of a chimpanzee troop is often the biggest, strongest male.

Female and young chimps have a lower rank than the males.

Who's Who?

A dominant male often stamps his feet and makes himself look very big to show he is the boss!

ON PATROL

A chimpanzee troop lives, feeds, and sleeps within one area. This area is called the troop's **territory**. Like army soldiers, the males in a troop **patrol** the **borders** of their territory. They walk around it to make sure that chimpanzees from other troops do not enter the area.

The males in a chimpanzee troop choose a territory that has enough food for the whole group. In **rain forests**, chimpanzees make a small territory because it is easy to find food there. In areas where there are few trees, chimpanzees choose a big territory to increase the space within which they can hunt for food. They use rocks and trees as markers to remember where the edges of their territory are.

Male chimps may patrol the troop's territory for hours at a time.

This male is at a lookout post. He is watching for **intruders** in the troop's territory.

Fight to Survive

When food is hard to find, males from a troop may form a hunting party. They attack another chimp troop and take land from it!

FINDING FOOD

Chimpanzees are **omnivores**. They eat mainly fruit, but also leaves, nuts, eggs, and insects. Chimpanzees are smart, and they know exactly where to look for food. They remember where the best fruit trees are and what time of year different fruits are ripe.

Some male chimpanzees also form teams to hunt small animals to eat, such as **antelope** or monkeys. They work together, like soldiers in an army. Some of the chimps chase **prey** through the forest. Some work as a team to block the prey's escape while other chimps in the group catch it.

These chimpanzees are working together to catch prey in the trees.

Ripe fruit makes up more than half of the food that chimpanzees eat.

Super Skills

Chimpanzees use medicines if they feel unwell. If they have an illness such as a stomachache, they eat special plants that help them to feel better.

FEEDING TIME

Chimpanzees feed for up to six hours a day! They usually find food such as fruit up high in trees, then sit in the tree to eat it. Chimpanzees get most of the water they need to survive from the fruit and plants that they eat.

Soldiers have can openers and forks, but chimpanzees make and use tools, too! They use stones to break open nuts at feeding time. They choose a long, thin stick to dip into an ant nest. The ants inside the nest crawl onto the stick. Chimps then pull out the stick and lick the ants from it. Chimps crush leaves to make them soft. They then use them as sponges to soak up drinking water from places that are hard to reach, such as rocky streams.

The alpha male eats first. The other chimps have to wait their turn!

Chimps use sticks as tools to help them to reach food.

Who's Who?

At feeding times, the alpha male usually eats first because he is the leader of the troop.

NEW RECRUITS

Female chimpanzees can have a baby at any time of year. Other chimps in the troop are interested in the new **recruit**, but only the mother takes care of it at first. When the baby is young, the mother carries it with her at all times and feeds it with milk from her body.

Females have around five babies in their lifetime.

Chimpanzees are very caring animals. Sometimes a young chimp's mother dies, leaving the chimp alone and **vulnerable** to attack from predators or starvation. In these cases, another chimp from the troop will often feed and care for the baby or young chimp so that it survives.

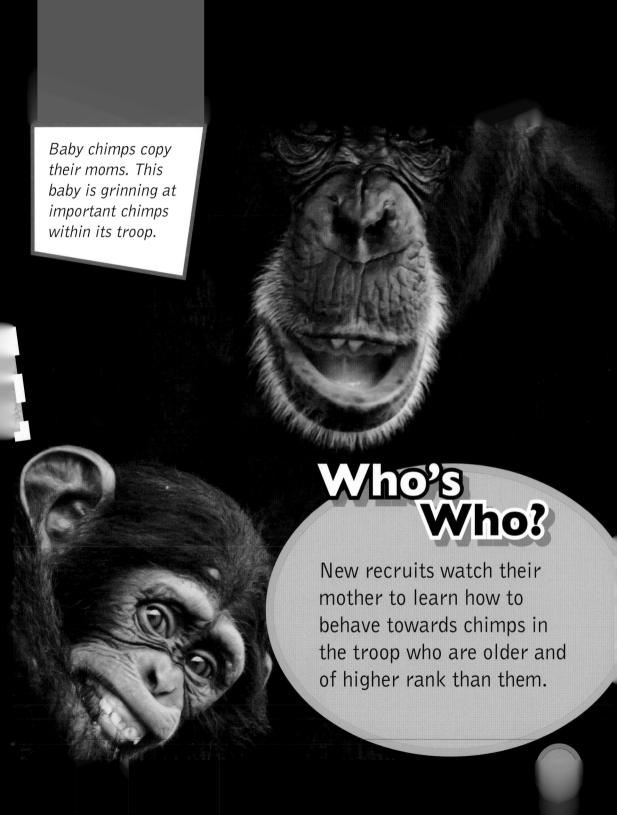

Baby chimps copy their moms. This baby is grinning at important chimps within its troop.

Who's Who?

New recruits watch their mother to learn how to behave towards chimps in the troop who are older and of higher rank than them.

TRAINING

New recruits have much to learn! Young chimps spend a lot of time following and watching the adults. This is how they learn important skills such as where to find food, how to hunt, and how to patrol the troop's territory.

Young chimpanzees chase each other and pretend to fight. This teaches the chimps important skills. Playing like this helps them learn how to fight and how to protect themselves when they are older. Play fighting and playing games such as "chase" makes young chimps strong. It also teaches them to run and climb safely within the troop's territory.

Young chimps form friendships as they play and learn together.

Older chimps often scold youngsters when they get something wrong!

Who's Who?

Young male chimps watch how the alpha male behaves. They learn to use **displays** like his to take control of their own small groups!

SENDING SIGNALS

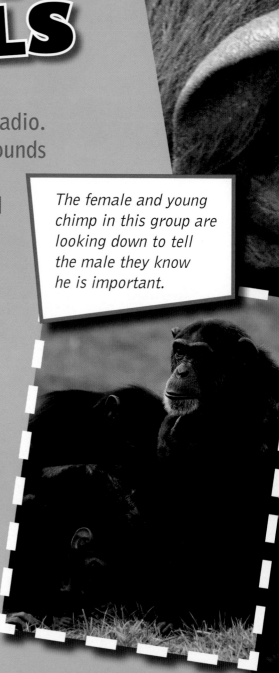

Soldiers send messages by radio. Chimpanzees make loud sounds that travel through the forest. Chimpanzees use a special call named a "pant-hoot" to tell other chimps where they are. Each chimpanzee makes a different pant-hoot sound so the troop knows exactly where each member is.

The female and young chimp in this group are looking down to tell the male they know he is important.

Chimpanzees also make faces to show their feelings and use hand signals to talk to each other. Alpha males clap hands or wave branches around to show that they are boss or to scold another chimpanzee.

Chimps open their mouth very wide to make loud pant-hoot calls.

Super Skills

Some chimpanzees in zoos can talk to their keepers in **sign language**. Others have even learned how to tap messages onto keyboards!

OFF DUTY

Chimpanzees travel and feed in the morning and evening. They rest in the middle of the day, when it is very hot. They rest on the ground or relax on branches, gripping on with their strong toes so they do not fall off.

Every evening, chimpanzees stop in a new place within their territory and set up a camp. They then make beds high in trees. First, they bend and twist branches together. Then they fill the bed with a mattress of leaves. Young chimps learn to make these leafy beds by watching their mothers. It is a useful skill for them to learn. Chimpanzees make a new bed to sleep in every single night!

A chimpanzee sleeping on a bed made of banana leaves.

Chimpanzees in a troop enjoy relaxing!

Fight to Survive

Chimpanzees make their beds high up in trees so they are safe from leopards and other predators while they sleep.

TEAM BUILDING

In an army, soldiers often play games together in their free time. Chimpanzees in a troop spend hours **grooming** each other. The chimpanzee who is grooming uses its fingers or lips to remove dirt, dead skin, or insects from the other chimpanzee's hair.

Chimpanzees groom each other to keep their hair clean and to get rid of insects. It is important to remove insects from the hair because they bite and can pass on diseases. Grooming is also a sign of friendship. It helps the chimps in a troop to feel safe and part of a team. Friendly chimpanzees also hold hands, kiss, stroke, and even tickle each other! Grooming brings chimps closer together.

Grooming reminds chimpanzees in a troop that they are part of a team.

Chimps hug other chimps to make them feel better after a fight.

Who's Who?

Chimps usually groom other chimps that are more important than them. Mothers also groom their babies.

TROOP CHANGES

Troops change when the alpha male of the group becomes too old and weak to be the leader. Other adult males then try to take over the troop. A new male becomes leader if he can show that he is the strongest male.

Male chimpanzees become the leader of a troop by defeating the old leader. They also fight any other male who tries to become the leader. Male chimps stay in the same troop for their whole lives. At eight to 10 years old, females become adults. Then they leave their troop to join another one.

Females leave their troop to **breed** with males from another troop.

24

After the age of 30, male chimps are no longer strong enough to lead their troop.

Who's Who?

When trying to become leader, a male makes friends with other chimps. If another male tries to defeat him, his friends then fight the male.

DEFENDING THE TROOP

Male chimpanzees sometimes attack chimps from other troops. They do this to steal land and food from the other troop. It is the duty of the males in a troop to stop intruders. They look out for intruders when they patrol their territory.

When males from a troop see intruders, they shout loudly and wave their arms in the air. This usually scares the enemy away. If the intruders do not leave, the males then work as a team to attack them. Fights can be very violent and male chimpanzees may be killed **defending** their troop.

The adult male chimps in a troop guard the young and the females.

Fight to Survive

When a chimpanzee sees a predator it screams a warning. The troop then usually has time to escape by climbing trees.

Leopards, and sometimes lions, catch and eat young, old, or injured chimps.

LAST TROOPS

Hunters take young chimps away in cages to sell as pets.

Many chimpanzee troops are in trouble. In the future they could even become **extinct** in the wild if their numbers continue to drop as quickly as they are falling at the moment.

Many chimpanzees are dying because of humans. People cut down forests so they can build highways, homes, and farms. There are then fewer trees for chimps to feed from and live in. People also kill chimpanzees to eat or to sell their meat. Some people even sell baby chimps as pets. Unless more is done to protect chimps, one day there may be no chimpanzee troops in the wild.

Troops of chimps can live happily together in reserves.

Fight to Survive

Reserves are areas of land where people are not allowed to cut down trees or harm animals. Chimpanzees can live here safely.

GLOSSARY

alpha (AL-fuh) An animal with the highest rank in a group.

antelope (AN-teh-lohp) Deerlike creatures that live in Africa.

apes (AYPS) Monkeylike animals that do not have a tail.

borders (BOR-derz) The edges of an area or territory.

breed (BREED) To mate with and have young with another chimp.

defeating (dih-FEET-ing) Winning against someone in a battle.

defending (dih-FEND-ing) Protecting against attack.

displays (dih-SPLAYZ) Shows put on to impress other chimpanzees.

dominant (DAH-mih-nent) The leader of a group.

extinct (ik-STINGKT) No longer existing.

grooming (GROOM-ing) Cleaning dirt or insects from hair.

intruders (in-TROOD-erz) People or animals that are unwelcome.

omnivores (OM-nih-vawrz) Animals that eat both plants and meat.

patrol (puh-TROHL) To move around an area to make sure it is safe.

predators (PREH-duh-terz) Animals that hunt other animals.

prey (PRAY) An animal that is eaten by other animals.

protect (pruh-TEKT) To keep safe.

rain forests (RAYN FOR-ests) Thick forests in hot, rainy places.

ranks (RANKS) The positions within an army or a group.

recruit (rih-KROOT) A new member.

reserves (rih-ZURVZ) Areas of land where animals are protected.

sign language (SYN LANG-gwij) Speaking by using hand signs.

territory (TER-uh-tor-ee) An area controlled by one animal group.

vulnerable (VUL-neh-ruh-bel) Weak, open to attack.

FURTHER READING

Albee, Sarah. *Chimpanzees*. Amazing Animals. New York: Gareth Stevens, 2010.

Moore, Heidi. *Chimpanzees*. Living in the Wild: Primates. Chicago: Heinemann-Raintree, 2012.

Owen, Ruth. *Chimpanzees*. The World's Smartest Animals. New York: Windmill Books, 2012.

WEBSITES

Due to the changing nature of Internet links, PowerKids Press has developed an online list of websites related to the subject of this book. This site is updated regularly. Please use this link to access the list: **www.powerkidslinks.com/aarmy/chimp/**

INDEX